I FIX ME

The Power of Self-Kindness

Dr. Keith L. Somerville

For permissions, bulk orders, or collaborations please send emails to *keithsomerville6@gmail.com*

Dr. Keith L. Somerville, Author

I Fix Me: The Power of Self-Kindness

ISBN: 979-8-218-59454-1 *(Paperback)*

Publishing Logistics, Auketria Manor
www.Themanordigital.com

Cover Design by Jessica Kalinga-Walker
www.Mybrandingstrategist.com

Interior Design by *Accuracy4sure*

Contents

CHAPTER I

WHAT'S SELF- KINDNESS REALLY ABOUT?

Philippians 3:12

> *[12] Not that I have already obtained all this, or have already arrived at my goal, but I press on to take hold of that for which Christ Jesus took hold of me.*

This book is not for you if you are uncomfortable with finding out who you are and not accepting what others think of you. If you are not okay with having a mirror held up to you by you so that you can see your flaws, cracks, blemishes, and character failures and see how all of it creates the beautiful mosaic that you are, then this book is definitely not for you. However, if you don't mind being uncomfortable, stretched, laughing, and crying, then you may have found something worth reading over and over again. Not that I already have obtained all of this and now sit on top of my personal high mountain, but I have discovered some people and things that I thought were pretty cool and wanted to invite you to join me on the self-kindness journey. As I write and you read, we will both grow and learn to see how incredible we are.

Found in the Holy Bible in the third chapter of the book of Philippians beginning at verse 12, Paul writes to the church in Philippi, "Not that I have already obtained all this or have already arrived at my goal." Let me start off by saying this is not a religious treaty or a new interpretation of any biblical philosophy. This is my attempt at seeking and sharing what I have found over the course of my life before and while currently serving the Church at the Village in Desoto Texas. As I write this book, I am in my 22nd year of full time Christian ministry. First, being an assistant pastor and later a senior pastor. I have planted ministries from scratch in Atlanta and Texas, and I have helped revitalize churches that were ready to close long before I showed up. I will lean on several of those experiences to explain how self-kindness and the lack of it has brought me and others to a place of self-loathing and failed relationships. I will also pull from 40 plus years of experiences with people from different faiths, religions, and of various cultural backgrounds. The goal is to make this body of work a mosaic in which everyone can locate themselves and apply these life experiences to their own. Of my firsthand experiences, I have found one truth to be consistent among them all. Whether you believe in something greater than yourself or you don't know what to believe, we all desire love. There are more books than there are libraries that speak to the issue of love, so I won't go into an in-depth study on the forms of love and how they are experienced. This is not that kind of book. But enough about what this book is not. What this book is about is showing you how I and others identified the immense power that can be tapped into by loving yourself and how to access the gift of self-kindness as you experience all that life has in store.

This book is also about discovering that you have had the ability to be kind to yourself and others all along and that if you do the work, the breakthroughs instore for you and everyone around you will be life altering. Finally, this book is about how pain and joy can coexist while pursuing how to love yourself.

Another thing that I have experienced over my years of engaging people of all walks of life is that there is no one answer to the question, "what is self-kindness?" Yet, at the same time, everyone wants to treat themselves better. Very few people I know make a choice to treat themselves poorly. Unfortunately, I once knew a woman who honestly sought ways to physically hurt herself. For reasons I still do not understand, she found intense pleasure in flogging, biting, and other explicit forms of what I would define as self-torture. I get certain people like alternative ways to be intimate, but this was different. But as crazy as it may sound, I still would say she wanted to treat herself more badly because for her it was the way she loved herself more. So, when I say everyone wants to love themselves better. I mean everyone. But still, I have found more people skilled at treating themselves harshly, carelessly, and unkindly more than being skilled at treating themselves with respect, care, and consideration. What I also found really interesting is though the practice of kindness and love for others can be found around the world, the lack of self-kindness and self-love can be found in greater abundance. It is not hyperbole to say I have found a lack of self-kindness in churches, synagogues, mosques, temples, wall street, rural and metropolises around the world. As I draft this book, there are so many mentors that I want to thank for helping me grow in personal understanding of what this all means. I can write an entire book just listing those persons. But the truth is, many of those mentors do not know how to read or write so they would never read the accolades in my work. So instead of leaving them out, I will just simply say, thank you for helping me in this pursuit of self-kindness and for giving me the space to share with everyone I meet.

CHAPTER II

OLD SCHOOL VS NEW SCHOOL KINDNESS

Isaiah 43:19

¹⁹ See, I am doing a new thing! Now it springs up; do you not perceive it? I am making a way in the wilderness and streams in the wasteland.

Let's start this chapter at the very beginning and say defining kindness is difficult. In my research, which includes asking a bunch of people older, smarter, and different from me in many ways what kindness is all about. And in my questioning, I have found there is no one definition that captures everything that being kind means. But guess what? If you think defining kindness is difficult, practicing kindness is a lot tougher. In a world so polarized because of race, religious certitude, gender misidentification, and a laundry list of other so called justifiable reasons, actually being kind in the world has always been extremely challenging. However, ask any person forty years or older than you and they would totally disagree. If they are like some of the seniors I know, they will tell you that in "their day" people were just naturally kind. It was no big deal for persons to talk to strangers and greet each other when they passed by in the streets.

Let them tell it, on any given day, look out your window and you would see neighbors borrowing sugar, playing with each other's children, and the front doors unlocked just in case unexpected guests dropped by. I remember once, my grandmother told me a story of how, after taking a long-needed shower she walked into her kitchen to see if the pie she had baked had cooled only to find a young boy sitting at her table burning himself eating the delicious treat. Her first reaction was shock, but then the young man "very politely" apologized for the intrusion and stated he could smell her dessert from outside and wanted to see if he could have a slice. Being the kind woman she was, she accepted his apology and cut him an additional piece. Now over the years, the specifics of that story changed, but her act of kindness despite the uninvited intrusion, remained the same. Now, I am not sure if this level of kindness was everyone's experience, but story after story I would hear similar tales from older adults. Amazingly, despite world wars, Jim crow violence, presidential assassinations, and many other atrocities committed during their youth, the older generation would swear that the world used to be a much kinder place. Where I cannot debate the legitimacy of the kinder past, I can say things have certainly changed. The world we experience now seems to be crueler than ever before. Murder rate continues to rise, employment continues to plumet, racial discrimination and microaggression are alive and thriving.

Overall disdain for people we deem different than us is evident everywhere we turn. While we are advanced in the treatment of illness, equitable health care for marginalized persons remains an issue. Spend ten minutes looking at any social media platform, and it is clear that people seem angrier and more self-involved than ever before. How many more posts can we endure where the message is "my life is better than yours" is the theme. Even worse than the lack of kindness towards each other, being kind to ourselves is practically nonexistent. Well maybe not nonexistent in your life, but let me share a personal story about how, even though I thought I loved myself, I came to realize that I didn't.

Seven years ago, I had a heart attack while working on an eighteen-wheeler truck in Texas style 95-degree heat by myself. BY MYSELF!!!! You may also ask, why does it have to be Texas style heat? Only a person who has never spent the summer in Houston would ask that question. Now to fully understand the madness of the event, I have to share that I am not a truck driver. Never been one, never rode in one, and never dreamed of becoming one. At the time, I was a church planter and as a part of the Sunday morning routine of planting a church, I had to pick up a trailer filled with chairs, sound equipment, instruments, and a bunch of other props to set up church before persons showed up. Me and a hand full of other volunteers committed to do the work every week so that for an hour and a half people could experience church in an otherwise old and uncomfortable middle school auditorium. But, to us that served, they were worth it. So, there I was about to pick up the truck when I realized that one of the tires was flat and would be unable to move. Did I call a tow company? Did I call a mechanic? Did I even call one of the faithful volunteers to come help me? Nope. That would have been an act of self-kindness, and I didn't know anything about that at the time. Instead, I decided to find a car jack and attempt to fix a truck alone. An hour later, flat tire still on the truck and my clothes drenched in sweat, I finally gave up and decided to go home and change. As soon as I got home, it hit me. I felt like I was on fire and my chest tightened up where I couldn't breathe. Fortunately for me, someone was able to get to the emergency room. When I arrived, they immediately hauled me to the back and got to work. Thankfully, the doctors were able to do what they needed to do, and I recovered. But this is where it gets interesting.

While spending three weeks in recovery, several doctors visited me. The cardiologist was the first. He explained to me that I had a clogged artery, and it was the primary cause of my attack. Then he began to ask me about the things I eat during the week. I proudly told him that I don't eat "sweets" and hate junk food. I went on to say I loved several types of steak, a cheese fanatic, and other assortments of high fat foods. Of course, I didn't know at the time that is what you called it. After listening, he said to me that most of the things I listed and the amounts were "bad" for me, and if I didn't stop eating that way, he would see me for my next cardiac event in a few months. Next, the doctor who was in charge of analyzing my cholesterol levels came and asked me a series of questions. After about thirty minutes of discussion, she repeated the same words. "That's bad for you." Next came the dietician. She was a specialist in working with diabetics.

Yes. I am a diabetic. After a lengthy discussion about the lack of vegetables in my diet and hearing the infrequency in which I ate was a major challenge, guess what she said? Correct! You are getting the overall theme of every conversation. After about the fourth doctor visited me, I pondered the reoccurring comment "That's bad for you." Then it hit me. I was bad for my health!!! No one else was to blame but me for what I ate. No one but me set the ridiculous work schedule I took so much pride in. No one but me knew all the right things to do, but consistently chose to do the opposite. I was bad for myself. By my decisions and actions, I did not like me, did not think much of me, and had become totally comfortable in treating myself unkindly. Now before you judge me too harshly, I want you to ask yourself some questions and see how you feel about yourself.

1. Typically, when it's time to eat, do you ask yourself, what will give your body the greatest benefit or what do you have a taste for?

2. Do you choose to work before or after your body gets the rest it needs to be fully functional?

3. When it is time to get dressed, do you take time to think about what your body will need to maintain optimum temperature, or do you worry about matching your tops with your bottoms and how others will look at your choice of outfit?

4. Do you only engage people who will help you improve or people who approve of you even when they know you are treating yourself poorly?

Depending on how you answer these questions you may hate yourself or at the very least are skilled at being very unkind to yourself. The other harsh reality is that many of the decisions we make concerning ourselves have more to do with how other people look at us, feel about us, or how they treat us, more than how we look at, feel about, or treat ourselves. Everything from the food we eat, the amount of work we do or the amount of time we take for ourselves depends on what others find appropriate for us. There are too many studies to share in this book where people have died because of people pleasing. Psychological studies are done on how stress increases. as we please other people and their thoughts about us. The next time you pick out your outfit, pause for a second and consider this, are you looking at you and thinking about how you look and feel about the clothes you are wearing? Or is the first thought that comes to mind more about how somebody else is going to like this outfit. If you are honest with yourself and can admit that many of your choices you have made are really not about you, but about other people's perception of you, then you really might hate yourself right now. Self-discovery that leads to self-kindness is difficult. There is no question about that. But the good news is, starting with this book, we will begin a journey exploring the many different ways we have been unkind to ourselves and then identify new ways to become more kind to the one who should be first in your life. You!

CHAPTER III

SELF-KINDNESS IS GETTING OVER YOURSELF

Probably one of the harshest things I heard as a child in middle school was when my class sweetheart looked me dead in my eyes and told me to "Get over yourself." Unfortunately for me, she didn't exactly explain what parts of me I needed to get over or what prompted the comment. So as any adolescent would do, I decided to choose which parts of me I needed to try to get over. And what does that mean anyway?! Now I have to warn you that being kind to yourself starts with you, but it does not end there. Learning how to be kind to yourself is not an exercise in narcissistic behaviors or to make you feel that you are better than anyone else. In fact, I believe the more kind you are to yourself, the more kind you will be to everyone else, and the more kind you are to others, the more kind, the people, who matter, will be kind to you. Did you catch that? I said the people that matter. The truth is, our journey to self-kindness does not end with us and all the major religions and faith "experts" agree, the end result of any work we do to improve ourselves results in others benefiting too.

The other truth is that not everyone will end up being kind to you. So don't try to use this book to influence the results of others behavior. That's manipulation and that's not why we are here. Along with many other things, we are called to be examples of how to love ourselves but like math, you can show others how to do calculus a thousand times, but it doesn't mean they will immediately understand it. Forgive those who don't get your journey and keep moving forward.

Merrion -Webster dictionary defines self as the union of elements (such as body, emotions, thoughts, and sensations) that constitute the individuality and identity of a person. Using this as a foundation of our understanding of the self, having an identity also implies that we need others in which to individuate ourselves. In plain language, without the existence of others, you would never know that you are an individual. The same is true with self-kindness. We can never know if we are truly being kind to ourselves without others experiencing your self-kindness. Have I confused you? Let me give you an exaggerated but simple example to make my point. Say for months you refused to take the time to take a bath. You created a life for yourself that considers hygiene as a waste of time. Before you laugh, not everyone in the world follows the same hygienic norms that you do. After a few months, one day unexpectedly, you finally smell the result of your lack of self-care.

Disgusted by your stench, you make up your mind to treat your nose better and take a bath. Not only do you use soap and water, but because you wanted to treat yourself better, you got a bath bomb, some body wash, and scented lotion for after the overdue scrub. Whether you know it or not, you have just practiced self-kindness and discovered not only is your nose thankful, but cognitive neuroscientist will tell you that what we smell has a positive impact on what we think about ourselves and how we behave. But here is what is really exciting. Other people will begin to also notice that you are taking care of yourself and begin to have a different reaction when you enter a room. Now, your self-kindness has not only made an impact on you but has made an impact on them. In turn their behavior towards you has changed and their behavior has positively impacted you.

When you are kind to yourself, everybody wins. But let me ask you a serious question now. When was the last time you were really kind to yourself? I mean you being really kind to you and only you. Before you answer, let me go ahead and confess again that you are talking with someone who is not truly kind to themselves. Or let me put it another way so that you don't think I am totally self-loathing. I am not consistently kind enough to myself to really say I practice self-kindness. If I am honest with myself, I am just starting to have this self-awareness of how much I have not been kind to myself. I have so many examples of awareness that I could fill up an entire book on discovering how I think about myself and who I really believe myself to be. Discovering that I had it all wrong for so exceptionally long has been gut wrenching but rewarding. Let me share a little about my own life to illustrate what I mean. Not too long ago, I went to a celebration at my old college alma mater. And without fail, every time I ran into somebody who knew me back then, they would say the same thing to me.

They would say, Keith, you look amazing! What's going on with you? What are you doing these days? Man, you look good! What's really happening in your life? And as I listened to each person say pretty much the same thing, I began to wonder what was I looking like before? What was I acting like back then? How was I as a person where they all saw some dramatic change? If you would have asked me, I would have told you that I was a happy guy in college and I thought I was easygoing and laid back. But, as I reflect on my past, I am beginning to discover that who I thought I was, was the story I told myself to hide the truth. Then, with the help of my wonderful therapist, I began to reflect on my days before college and how I looked at myself as a child and teenager. I began to explore a lot of the decisions I made and how I treated myself.

I removed other people from the reflections and focused entirely on me and pondered the things that I ate, the people that I chose to hang around with, and the habits that I picked up. And the truth is much of my early life was filled with self-loathing, self-hatred, and self-abuse. Along with a number of other mental, emotional, and even spiritual struggles that I waged on myself, I created an environment where I was always down on myself. And so even as I author this book, I think about how I treated myself versus how I'm treating myself now. I used to practice this half-kindness philosophy. I now see what they saw and the importance of practicing complete self-kindness. To start with complete self-kindness, we must accept that self-kindness is the foundation of transformation. Without it, we will forever remain the wounded, fearful, self-loathing person many of us have become. When we are kind to ourselves, we treat our bodies differently. When we are kind to ourselves, we think differently. When we are kind to ourselves, we chose different people to engage with. When we are kind to ourselves, we treat everyone differently and the moments that we spend alone are filled with wonder, tears, laughter, and excitement. Sense of newness fills our being along with some fear of the unknown. But overall excitement of the possibilities fills your life. In contrast, self- kindness not openly shared becomes a ticking time bomb waiting to explode. If we do not ignite it and let it explode outwardly, it will simply implode and what others see if a self-involved mess.

My friend Greg is a wonderful example of an imploding self-kindness bomb. As a part of his journey towards self-kindness, Gregg began to shop for himself. He bought some really nice outfits with all the appropriate accessories. Because he made a modest living, he was initially cautious in the amount of money he spent. As he began to go out with friends, they noticed his change of dress and the confidence he began to develop. However, anytime someone would complement him on his attire, he would respond with self-loathing. Instead of saying thank you and explaining that he was trying to love himself more, he downplayed it. He either ignored their accolades or turned them into insults. After a while, his friends stopped commenting on his appearance altogether. This made Greg even more anxious about his appearance and he started to buy more expensive outfits in hopes they would complement him again. What started out as an exercise in self-care turned into him being stressed about his finances, anxiety about impressing others, and becoming bitter. Gregg did one thing right. He desired to go from self-complimenting to others recognizing his progress. The challenge, however, was that he didn't know how to go from a soloist to being a part of a team of persons who would help him in his self-kindness journey.

CHAPTER IV

SELF-KINDNESS-
A TEAM SPORT

Psalm 139:14

> *14 I praise you because I am fearfully and wonderfully made; your works are wonderful; I know that full well.*

Self-kindness also becomes a balm we use in order to heal some of the wounds of the past and also protects us from having similar wounds in our present. Do you remember the movie Shallow Hal? That movie had a lot of great themes. Spoiler alert. It was about a man who had a perception of beauty where pretty much everyone he saw was ugly in his eyes. After going to a therapist, he was hypnotized in believing that people were beautiful. This was the surface transformation. The real transformation happened when he realized he was ugly on the inside and what he saw in others was only a reflection of how he saw himself. At least that is what I got from the movie. Someone once said that the hate we have for others is only a reflection of the hate we have for ourselves. I fully agree with that. Let me share a story to illustrate the point. A guy I knew for years used to body shame me and others. He was a chubby kid himself, but when it came to others, he was relentless with the insults.

Years later, I ran into him, and we went out to talk. During our conversation, he shared with me after years of extensive therapy, he could admit that every morning as a youth he would look at himself in the mirror and hate his body. He hated it so much that he would point out parts of his body and tell hateful jokes about himself. Later, when he got around others, his insults towards us were really just a spillover about how he felt about himself. Later, when he began to treat himself kindly, he began to see himself in a kinder way and also discovered how badly he treated us because of his own self-hate. As he became kinder to himself, he also saw others differently and treated them differently. He had a Shallow Hal experience all his own. That is how self-kindness transforms and heals. In the passage at the beginning of this chapter, Theologians believe David wrote this Psalm to encourage priests to keep praising God for what God did in creating humanity. It is also an incredible verse about self-awareness. But not the typical self-hate, self-loathing, or negative thoughts we typically have of ourselves. In this translation David calls being human 'wonderful." The Greek word for wonderful also means to pay remarkably close attention. The image here is that God took his time with you. He was extremely focused and knew everything that he wanted to create when he formed you. How amazing is that? You are the intentional creation of the God who creates all things.

Let me pause to encourage you. If you're going through a trying time as you are trying to practice self-kindness. If you are finding it hard to actually read that you are wonderful, extraordinary, and the intentional creation of a God who loves you. Keep going!!! I often tell people working hard is not hard when you're actually working at it. It is only when we think about how hard it is and not actually working at it that it seems hard. The same is true with working hard at self-kindness. The more we actually try to be kind to ourselves by seeing ourselves as God sees us, the easier it will become. There is this popular series on Tik Tok where this woman is talking to black men and reminding them how wonderful they are. It is intended to uplift black men. Especially those who may not receive affirmation anywhere else.

But if I am honest, it is extremely difficult to watch if you are not used to being affirmed. It is challenging work to listen. But then again, it's not hard. I only think it is. If that is also you. Keep Going! You are not alone and the more you work at it, the more others will begin to come into your life and work at it with you. This is a cause and affect progression of self-kindness. Later on, we will go into more detail about the cause and effect of self-kindness.

But for now, I want to encourage you to get excited about the journey. Get excited about treating yourself better. Get excited about discovering new things about yourself. Get excited about finding out that you are quite amazing, beautiful, intelligent and that there is more to you than you can even imagine. I am a part of a healing group that follows many of the same steps as Alcohol Anonymous. By the way, there are hundreds of distinct groups like that. So many groups have been formed using their model it blows the mind. I, like so many other anonymous groups believe the steps work if you work them. Meaning if you try to move forward through them with a sincere effort, forgiveness, and patience, you will see results. In my group we first begin our conversations by declaring we are in recovery for a common issue and then state our first name.

So that is what I am doing now. Hello. My name is Keith, and I do not practice self-kindness well. I am just beginning to realize that I have been addicted to treating myself poorly and that I have become skilled at always putting everyone else's needs above my own. The good news is that neither you nor I have to continue to treat ourselves that way. We can move beyond self-denial, fruitless sacrifice, self-abuse, and maltreatment for a full life of love, freedom, and agency over our own emotions. But again, this is not purely a selfish endeavor to take care of yourself, I want to also show you how your self-kindness practice will also help others.

Imagine for a moment you had a coworker you didn't particularly like. Not that you disliked them, but you never were available to get to know them beyond the occasional smile and hello. Then one day you decided to do something nice for them. You noticed that they often forget to bring lunch to work and as a result only eat snacks they find around the office to get them through the day. You also notice that as the day goes on, they get increasingly irritable and more unpleasant to be around. They go from a morning hello and smile, to an afternoon of barely acknowledging your existence and turning into a school yard bully that you do everything in your power to avoid. This is probably the reason you don't engage them at the office. So, one day you decide in the spirit of kindness to take the time to find out what they like to eat and during your break one day you buy them a meal and surprise them with it. Now imagine their surprise and huge smile because of your thoughtful action. Instantly, their demeanor changes and there is a shifting that takes place in the office. As you hand them the delicious treat, you see their behavior not only changed that day but days afterwards as they reflect on your kindness towards them. Your random thoughtful act of kindness has now shifted their behavior and probably the atmosphere of the work environment. Now, imagine that it was not your coworker, but you, who took the time to reflect how you feel when you miss lunch. Reflect about how your attitude may increasingly get worse as the day goes on and then notice how not too many coworkers engage you towards the end of those long, and hungry days. Then think about what meal you like to eat and one day during your break you brought yourself your favorite meal and enjoyed it. That's self-kindness step one.

Taking time to reflect on your needs, the things you enjoy, and then taking action to meet the need. What would the rest of your workday look now? Would you have renewed energy? Would your stress level decrease because you nourished your body? Next, imagine that everyone notices your friendly disposition. They begin to comment that your energy is electrifying, and they start asking you questions about your diet and exercise routine. You laugh with each other as you shared you just decided to treat yourself to your favorite meal. Now look at how wonderful it is that the work environment shifted. Who knows? Someone may see what you did for yourself and decide to do the same. Now you have created a culture of self-care disciples eager to feel better and create a better work environment. That's how self-kindness effortlessly becomes community kindness.

Like many siblings, my brothers and I have had a serious rivalry that could compare to the Hatfield's and McCoy's for most of our childhood. And like many sibling rivalries, as I got older, it became harder and harder to explain why there was such anger and frustration between my brothers and I. Counselors have produced several reasons and written volumes on why brothers and sisters are at each other's throats in their childhood. They have theorized everything from inborn jealousy of anyone close to them to rationalizing that fighting your sibling is the safest way to act out personal aggression without retaliation that can cause us harm. Now, I am not a psychologist or a philosopher, but after years of experiencing sibling rivalry personally, I consciously sought healing from my turbulent past by wanting to figure out why it happened in the first place. Over the years, it became clear, in my life, there was not a simple answer to why I had such vitriol towards my brothers. There were actually several layers that I had to peel back to understand. The good news is that lessons of forgiveness and kindness was on the other side of the work. As a result, we have an incredible relationship today.

The same is true for you. If you put the effort in and endure the pain and struggle that comes from doing the self-reflective work, waiting for you on the other side is a community of love, forgiveness, and understanding. I cannot say for sure, but perhaps my journey towards self-kindness began with an incident when I was ten years old with my five-year-old brother. Till this day, I cannot tell you why, but I knew I was jealous of my grandmother's treatment of Michael during our formative years. It felt like the sun and moon rose and set on him and he was flawless in every way possible. My therapist believed it could be because my grandmother was his biological father's mother, and she loved him like she loved her own son.

The other widely held belief is that I felt that way because as the only child for five years, I had my mother all to myself. Then he came along, and I got 50% of her time and my grandmother gave him everything else. But who knows? All I know is that it felt like anytime he would wine or cry, my grandmother would come running full speed in the direction he was located, pick him up and hold him close to her. I would often stand there, watch her nurse his pretend wounds, and rock him back to a smile. But when I got hurt. The response was completely different. There were no all-out sprints, no drop everything and come check on me, no sweeping me up from the floor or cuddles until I was soothed. I did not receive the same response, and I believed with all my heart it was because he was her favorite. And so, one day, deciding that I would pay her back for what seemed like years of mistreatment and favoritism, I concocted a plan that would satisfy all my adolescent pain and anger. Imagine this. It was a typical day, and my grandmother was in the kitchen preparing a meal for my brothers and me to eat. While she was preoccupied preparing our food, my brothers and I played in a different room about fifty feet from where she was located. At just the right moment in a McIver like fashion, I took one end of my belt and tied it to a chair. Then, with the other end of the belt, I extended it and created a make-shift apparatus to trip her. The diabolical trap was set, and all that was left was to pinch my little brother so he would give the loudest cry and send my grandmother running.

When my grandmother heard the yell of anguish, she dropped everything and ran full speed into the room and my trap. I will never forget the sound she made when she flew into the air, landed on her face, and chipped her tooth. I thought that was the funniest thing I had ever seen. I finally had the satisfaction of knowing I got the vengeance I deserved. However, what I didn't realize at that moment was not only did I trip my grandmother and get my vengeance, but simultaneously, I was tripping and hurting my father's mother. If you have never hurt someone's mother before, let me warn you now, that is a gravely, unwise decision. I remember the look on my father's face when she told him what I had done. In fact, I still have nightmares about it. Not only was I unkind to my grandmother, father's mother, and my brother, but my actions had clearly shown that I was perfectly fine with being unkind to myself. Following what felt like a life sentence of grounding, chores, and examples on how not to spare the rod and spoil the child, I also had to endure my mother's almost daily opportunity to teach me a life lesson.

My mother was a master at teaching me lessons that, at the time, I thought were gibberish but, later in life, would flood my thoughts and give me direction. Her lessons were so simple yet impactful and her words often served as guideposts throughout life. I once told my Religion professor that my first experience with the Holy Spirit had her voice because before I experienced the Spirit, she was always in my ear about right and wrong. Well, on the day I tripped my grandmother, I recall my mother sitting me down and saying, "I need to be more kind." Like many other times in my adolescent years, at the time they were only words to me. But as I got older and began to experience life, I would reflect on those words and wonder if I knew what kindness really was. Sure, I've heard it, and, like you, I have watched countless movies that would attempt to portray it, but did I know what it meant to be kind to someone else. And more than just knowing it intellectually, I wondered if I could see it exercised in everyday life.

So that's what I have begun to do. Without her and many others, I would not have really understood what kindness was and later how kindness would be one of the greatest gifts I would receive from and also share with others. In fact, when I first began to pray about drafting this book, I wasn't really sure why I thought it needed to be said. I often felt alone, dejected, misunderstood, and treated poorly. However, as I continued to live and experience love from others, I saw clearly that this book would be about growing through those times and learning the power of kindness that we all possess. I hope that at the end of this book, you will see the true power of kindness in you and others. To be more kind to yourself and others is a family affair, and how you share your power to be kind with others can change the world.

CHAPTER V

TO BE OR NOT TO BE KIND

Let me ask you a question. On the scale of 1 to 10. How compassionate and accepting do you think you are to yourself? I am at one of my favorite coffeeshops and this young lady just shared with me that my approach to the subject matter is too soft. Ha! It's a book on being kind and she said she would rather me be more abrupt and almost rude in my approach. Now before you answer my question, let's talk first about what compassion and acceptance might be. After we explore those two words in particular, we will then put ourselves in between them and be able to discover whether or not we truly have been compassionate and accepting of ourselves. About two years ago I began a practice called Transcendental Meditation. An article written in Science Direct defined Transcendental Meditation as a mantra-based technique popularized by Maharishi Mahesh Yogi. It is an effortless procedure for allowing the excitation of the mind to settle down until a state of calmness is reached.

This practice strives for a state of alertness with relaxation and no object of thought or perception. It has been described as a state in which the person is aware of his or her consciousness and its unbounded nature. Let's try to practice that right now so you understand what I am talking about. First, find a space where you can sit in uninterrupted silence for no less than ten minutes. Next, remove any jewelry you may have on or anything in your hand. Next, I want you to find a comfortable position and count ten breaths. While focusing on your breath, think about a positive affirmation. That's it! Do this for ten minutes and don't worry if your mind wanders. Allow the thought to play out and once you recognize that you have wandered, gently return back to the affirmation. This single practice over the course of six months has helped me to increase my awareness of the things I think about, how my body feels, and the spaces that I am in. It has also helped me recognize how easily I am distracted. Often, during meditation, instead of focusing on the positive words of affirmation, I think about trivial and negative things I speak to myself. For example, one day, I chose to meditate on the phrase "I am loved." I got into my special room, burned my favorite candle, put on noise reduction earphones to drown out any passing cars, and started saying my phrase. I had my breathing down, and I was completely still in the moment. However, after about two minutes of repeating that same phrase, out of nowhere I found myself thinking about people at work and the tasks that waited for me. From there, I went into a tailspin about what I was going to wear, when I'm going to get my haircut, how I needed some new adidas, and several other meaningless thoughts that did not affirm that I was loved.

But again, the beauty of this type of practice is that once you are aware that you have been distracted, you are instructed to gently go back to the positive phrase you've chosen. So that's what I did. A few more minutes passed by, and once again I started criticizing myself because of the things that I had left undone. At this point, I have been practicing now for close to two years and I realize I am only scratching the surface of being willing to look at myself in a completely positive light. There is something in me that makes me default to negative thoughts. Whether it was an experience in my background, in my past, my present, or thoughts of the future, my mind drifts to a place of criticism. The good news though, the more I practice, the better I become at recognizing it and shifting my thoughts to things that affirm me and builds me up emotionally, mentally, and physically. It's not about how much I think about the flaws. It's about celebrating those times I am aware of what I am doing and replace it with something fabulous about myself. That is being compassionate. Acceptance, however, is different from compassion. Where compassion might be you being tender towards yourself, acceptance is paying attention to the areas in your life desperately needing to be worked on. Often, when people tell you that you have to learn to accept where you are in life, they fail to tell you what that means. First, let me congratulate you on the fact that if you are still reading this book, you are at the very least on the surface of self-awareness. There is no acceptance without awareness about where you are right now and reading this far means you are aware that you have some work to do. Let me give you an example of what I mean by awareness. I have a friend who, every year, takes his family on an intercontinental trip by renting a Winnebago and traveling to different states. His goal is to take his family to visit every state in the U.S. Every summer he packs everyone up and off they go. Sometimes they take planes to certain states and drive to the neighboring states to enjoy the local sites. My friend, however, has one interesting quirk. He doesn't like using GPS. Though he is still young, he loves the old school method of using a paper map to get to his desired location.

Normally, it is a fun activity for everyone. However, every now and again, he gets horribly lost. To make things worse, he does not realize (or admit) he is lost until hours after he is supposed to arrive at his destination. The good news is as soon as he recognizes he is lost; he is able to track to the place where it went wrong and get back on the right path. The same is true

26

with many of us who have never practiced self-kindness. We have spent a lot of our time, energy, and resources headed in one direction, only to finally realize we are lost. Lost to the people who love us. Lost to the opportunities that awaited us. Lost to becoming our best selves. It is not until we practice self-kindness that we even become aware that we have been lost and doing life completely wrong. But when we make up our minds to be kinder to ourselves, we also begin to recognize the things in our lives that we should do differently.

Let me give another example. A dear friend of mine recently found out that he has high cholesterol. His cholesterol was so high, that his doctor said bluntly, I am surprised you were able to make it to my office. You should have died on the way to see me. That's how bad it was. What was more alarming is when the doctor asked him when was the last time he saw a healthcare provider and the type of diet he had. My friend had not seen a doctor in years and his diet consisted of steaks, porkchops, and a side of bacon. Sounds familiar? Like a good doctor should, the physician took time to make him aware of how his diet was killing him. That's when the acceptance of where he was in life began.

By becoming aware of how his life choices and eating habits were affecting him, he also now had a decision to make. He could either continue to ignore the doctors warning and his newfound awareness or he could do something about it and possibly extend his life. My friend decided to be kind to himself and make the necessary changes. Accepting where you are also helps you see that where you are now is not where you have to always remain. As I have said a few times so far, this process is not a get fixed quick program. In fact, there is no fixing you. On this journey, you will have opportunities to discover, reflect, evaluate, and make decisions. Then as we continue, you may find that previous decisions no longer fit. That is what this journey is about. It's about finding out what you believed may no longer apply as you grow. But before growth, there has to be awareness.

CHAPTER VI

THE IN BETWEEN TIME

Deuteronomy 30:19

> [19] *This day I call the heavens and the earth as witnesses against you that I have set before you life and death, blessings, and curses. Now choose life, so that you and your children may live.*

Those who practice self-kindness will always find themselves at some point in the "in between" stage of the process. Part of the journey of self-kindness is learning how to balance acceptance and compassion. Here is a diagram to illustrate what I mean:

The first line shows an example of a balanced life. Point A is awareness. Point B is you. Point C is compassion.

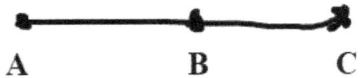

A   B   C

Notice how even the not so straight line is. The less than perfect line represents life. Though it is never completely straight, the goal with self-kindness is to make our lives as balanced as possible through an ongoing journey from awareness to compassion. Chances are, you will never be completely done being compassionate, because you will never stop discovering things about yourself to be compassionate about. But your life will be so much more balanced as you learn and then love yourself. Unfortunately, for many of us, our life looks either like Diagram B or C.

Diagram B shows us when we are just starting to be aware of the areas in our lives that need awareness and compassion.

A   B   C

Unfortunately, for many of us, we remain almost at the starting point of our journey towards self-kindness because we get stuck in the pain of realizing our areas of growth or have become comfortable with the routine of self-loathing. From this disadvantage point, compassion seems too high of a mountain to climb. We convince ourselves that we don't have enough time to achieve our goals of being happy and as a result, we never get to experience the incredible healing power of self-compassion. Instead, we have allowed fear, anger, or insecurity to keep us at the beginning of our journey. Years ago, I did a counseling session with a young woman who had become aware that she only dated guys who took from her and never gave her the love and respect she freely gave. The challenge for her was that the same men who took from her also gave her a sense of security because they stayed around to take. In order to move from the relationships that was hurting her, she also had to move from the feelings of security she received from having them around. In the end, she decided to stay where she was with an unbalanced life because the thought of being alone was too scary for her to imagine.

Diagram c illustrates another type of imbalanced self-loathing life.

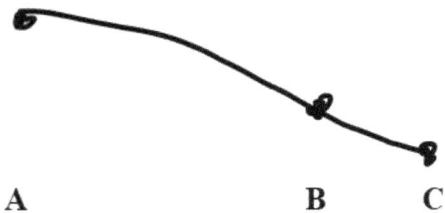

A   B   C

This diagram shows that we have mastered the art of becoming aware and we are well on our way to being compassionate to ourselves. We quickly identify where we need to grow and do the things that we need to do to address the new awareness quickly. We become skilled at developing new habits to meet the need and we celebrate ourselves excessively. The challenge arises, however, when we don't spend enough time trying to understand our new awareness. We are so focused on moving up, we neglect taking the time to understand what we have already achieved and how to continue to master the discipline that got us this far. Becoming aware of your areas of growth not only requires guts and grit, but it also requires time and reflection to learn where your growth areas originated and how it has affected you and others throughout your life. Without doing the necessary work of understanding why you have spent your life treating yourself poorly, you are destined to return to old behaviors. Sometimes as quickly as you rose from them. The challenges we face present differently depending on <u>who you are right now and</u> the path that led you back to your starting point may be a different, but the same self-loathing, defeated attitude will pop up and hurt you again.

Years ago, a great friend of mine had lost about 85lbs by mandate of his doctor. He had lost the weight quicker than anyone I had ever known, and he looked as great as he said he felt. When I asked him how he did it, he said he gave up ice cream. Max was an ice cream-aholic. No judgement, but he ate tubs of ice cream daily for as long as I knew him. It was his thing to do no matter what else he ate. In fact, for years, he was known as the ice cream man though he never drove a truck with a jingle. Unfortunately for Max, though he dropped the weight quickly, he never took the time to think about why he was addicted to ice cream. He never asked himself if there were triggers in his life that made him eat so much over the years. He never took the time to understand his why for he had a daily habit of ice cream consumption. He just celebrated the fact that the weight was gone. To replace the ice cream addiction, he got really into cheeseburgers. Guess what? As a result of his newfound cheeseburger love and to his dismay, a year later, not only did he gain all the weight he lost back, but he also gained even more. Then take Steve. Steve had been unhappily married for 15 of his 20 years of marriage. One day, he finally became aware that the reason he had been unhappily married. But instead of insisting for a divorce, he did the work to find out he was unhappily married mostly because he was unhappy with himself. Unfortunately for Steve, once he became aware of the parts of himself he needed to work on, he didn't just work on him, he became angry with his spouse. And began to tear down his relationship. He used phrases like, "I love myself enough not to eat your food anymore." I love myself enough to find hobbies I can do alone." "I love me enough to not listen to any critiques you may have." Steve knew he wanted to work on his self-esteem and self-kindness, so he began to do more activities he enjoyed. But because he didn't take the time to understand his role in how his lack of selfcare affected his wife, he ended up getting a divorce anyway. His divorce led to depression, which led to him treating himself poorly in other ways. Unlike Mark, he took time to understand himself, but instead of working with his wife on his newfound self-compassion, he weaponized it and used it to cause harm to himself and his relationship.

Self-kindness is finding the balance between awareness and compassion. It is learning about yourself today by exploring your past, creating a vision for your future, and taking time to enjoy all the many layers of your life right now as they unfold. I want to invite you to do an exercise that I learned from Matt Haig called, the Why Game. I'm not sure he called it that, but let's go with it. I want you to write down one challenge you have that you know keeps you from being kind to yourself. Then ask yourself why that challenge exists. Then ask yourself what is the "why" of your answer. Continue to do that until you no longer have a reasonable answer to the question of why. When you are done, see if what you have uncovered has anything to do with the original challenge. Often, we find that the thing we think stops us from being kind to ourselves and others has nothing to do with what we thought was really the cause. The other absolutely wonderful discovery is that you have now created a road map that you can use to stay away from the end result caused by self-loathing. As a child, I remember reading the story of Hansel and Gretel. At the time, I had no idea that it was really a horror story filled with victims. But if you know the story, you know the children used breadcrumbs to mark a path as they traveled further and further into the unknown wilderness. The idea was to leave a trail that they could follow back to their original location. The goal of the Why Game however is the exact opposite. We leave breadcrumbs or markers as we travel into the unknown world of self-discovery not so we can find our way back, but so that we can recognize that if we are not careful, we will end up right back to the place we told ourselves we would never return. There is one thing, however, the old fable and our journey does have in common.

Like the children, you will experience various emotions on this journey. Some will be of extreme joy and sometimes you will be downright terrified because you don't know exactly how you feel learning more about yourself. But one unescapable truth during this time is that you will learn to pay attention to your emotions. I invite you at this point to close the book, set a timer for five minutes, and feel every emotion you are feeling right now. Are you feeling the way you are because of what you read so far? Or were you distracted by something that caused an emotion that you didn't even know you were feeling until right now? Whatever you are feeling right now, doing this before you continue, will help you check back in and get focused on the material ahead of you.

CHAPTER VII

EMOTIONAL WARFARE

Romans 7:19

> *19 For I do not do the good I want to do, but the evil I do not want to do—this I keep on doing.*

Bad News. Self-Kindness requires a level of emotional intelligence many of us do not have. In 1996, one of my favorite shows "Everybody Loves Raymond" aired. Till this day, it was to me, one of the funniest sitcoms I ever watched. Now don't get me wrong, there have been several incredible comedies that have aired before and after Ray Romano's successful situational comedy. But for me, what made this one of the funniest shows was the irony. Ray Barone, played by Comedian Ray Romano was irony personified. Though the show was called Everybody "Loves Raymond," the truth is it seemed everybody always had a problem with him, and he had a problem with everyone else. Masked in quick witted humor, Ray was a miserable guy. His wife could never seem to get anything right, his children were almost nonexistent in his life, his parents constantly nagged him, and his brother was an abundant source of criticism for everything he did.

The show would have been more appropriately titled "Everybody Hates Raymond." Beyond all of their criticism, Ray had the most complaints. He complained about everything from his relationship to his sports job. It seemed like every week, the smallest thing would upset him. On top of all of that, I don't think he realized how miserable he was. For me, that is the definition of emotional unintelligence. If I am honest, I sometimes wonder if I am emotionally intelligent as well. Yes, I know this is a book about self-kindness, but before I can really address what it means to be kind to yourself, I have to do some self-purging. So here we go! Let's start with my teenage years. I do not know about you but growing up I was an emotional imbecile. Especially when it came to relationships. I was a complete ignoramus about what I was feeling most times and how to express it to others. What is worse than that? Trying to start a new relationship with someone without healing from the past hurt first. I can write an entire book on how bringing an eighteen-piece baggage set to your new relationship causes extreme harm to you and others and is the exact opposite of what self-kindness is all about. I remember the first time I learned that the hard way. I had just come out of a long relationship, and I thought the quickest way to get over her was to find someone new. I told myself that a new person meant that I too, would be new and that together we would have completely new experiences. So as quickly as I could, I met someone and went on a date. One date led to another and so on.

There we were getting to know one another's interest, hobbies, favorite movies, and having a wonderful time. Then out of nowhere, she asked about my previous relationship. It was a fair question and with a more emotionally intelligent person, perhaps it could have led to some really enjoyable conversation and insight into one another's preferences. Instead, however, a totally unhealed Keith used that moment to sound like a lyric from Sade's song, "Somebody Already Broke My Heart." Almost word for word I said,

"I've been torn apart so many times.
I've been hurt so many times.
So be careful and be kind.
Somebody already broke my heart."

From there I told this undeserving woman play by play about how my ex ripped my heart out. I replayed every argument, disagreement, misunderstanding I could think of. The more I shared about my past, the more emotional I became. I went from chuckles to anger back to laughing. Then guess what? From the very depths from which I shared; I busted out in tears. And not the cute one tear drops from movies like Hope Floats, but the Jerry McGuire "You complete me" full on cry. I was an emotional hurricane destroying everything in its path. Especially any hope of a healthy relationship with this innocent bystander. Needless to say, that was the very last time I saw her. She blocked my number, and I think may have actually moved away so that I could not find her. It was that bad. Someone once wrote, "emotional intelligence refers to an integration in the war between emotion and rationality." Whoever wrote that nailed it in my opinion. Being emotionally intelligent feels like a war going on inside of us and the goal is to have both sides of yourself live in harmony. Whether it is a relationship, friendship, or even work interaction, there is always a battle happening between what you feel and how you process whatever is happening at the time. For example, I really hate when I have to meet with the supervisor at my job. The main reason is because, for whatever reason, supervisors I have had did not like to let me know why they wanted to meet with me until I got to the meeting. No agenda? No cliff notes. Nothing! From the moment I would receive the notice of the meeting, something on the inside of me would begin to grumble, stomach turn, and I would begin to develop serious anxiety.

The other thing that almost always happened was that I would create scenarios in my mind about why my supervisor wanted to meet. I can't really tell you when this paranoia began for me, but I can say with confidence that every time someone of authority wanted to speak with me, I immediately go down a rabbit hole of despair. Thinking that I've done something wrong is only the beginning. Even when I know that my work is great, I'm on time, and that my performance is above average, I find myself questioning everything that I do. Despite high praise, there is still something on the inside of me that invents the worst possible scenario. "Yup! I was late three months ago and now my career is over, and my dreams unfulfilled. Before I realize it, my emotions have just kicked the mess out of any rational thoughts I may have had. That's emotional warfare for me. I wonder what yours is. In fact, I want to invite you to stop here and grab your journal and write down three known triggers that leads to emotional warfare in your life. After you are finished, let me encourage you and share the good news. There is an opportunity in the midst of all emotional battles to learn and grow. You can take the negative emotions you are feeling and use it to benefit you. Not later when you are old and gray. Right now! Whenever we are experiencing emotions, especially the negative emotions that we all feel, there is still something positive that can come from it. The key to using those emotions for your benefit is what we are calling self-awareness.

Self-awareness is a catchy way of saying, paying attention to you. Not the things that caused the emotion, but everything that is happening to you as you are experience whatever emotional is happening.

Earlier, I shared with you my experience with previous supervisors and how it caused me major anxiety. Here I am not focusing on the actions that led to my feelings. I am paying close attention to everything that is happening in me that I called "anxiety." Things like a faster heartbeat, stomach cramps, and sweating are examples of what I noticed is physically happening. Thoughts like how my supervisors face would look, what I see myself saying, the room that I believe the unwelcome news will take place in are also important to note. Everything you notice in the moment matters and the more you become skilled at watching yourself, seeing yourself, and then taking care of yourself, the more you will grow in emotional intelligence and use the information to better yourself for yourself. We do this by taking several small steps.

Step One: Recognize that your body has a mind of its own.

The second step to understanding yourself is understanding that the emotional part of the experience is only part of the ways our bodies gather the necessary information in the decision-making process. Let me say that another way. When you feel fear, sadness, or any other emotion, that is only part of the information you need to make a clear decision. What you are thinking or feeling in the moment is never the ending of understanding everything happening in the moment. It is in many ways, just the beginning of total self-awareness. Once we recognize that our emotions are only part of the information that our body receives in the decision-making process, then we can begin to look for the other pieces of valuable information. One of the funniest commercials ever aired was the Snickers "Hangry" campaign. The top commercial being the one where Betty White was the angry personal. Look it up and thank me later. Basically, the point of the commercial was to convince people that they are not themselves when hungry. The emotional outburst in itself is not explained. Only that it may be connected to hunger, dehydration, and malnutrition that ultimately impacts more than just our emotions. Knowing that is also a form of emotional intelligence. It is the ability to recognize that your feelings are only part of your entire self.

How many times have you found yourself in situations where you based your next response or your reaction only on how you were feeling? That person made me mad, and so I'm going to respond in an angry manner. That person said something that offended me and now I'm sad and so I'm going to defend myself and say something sad or do something which causes them to be hurt as well. But what would it look like if when we felt sad about a situation, we would stop and ask ourselves why we are sad? Not just the situation but what else is happening with me that is making me be sad? Getting that answer and incorporating it into other pieces of information will help in your decision to either stand there and listen to that person or retaliate.

Let's use our imagination and practice that now. A good friend walks up to you and says out of nowhere, "You sure are looking chubby right now." That's it. What if instead of breaking down and crying or cussing them out, we took time to think about how and why we are feeling these emotions and ask ourselves some questions? What is going on with them that they needed to open the conversation this way? What is the best response I can make to that statement that would benefit them and me at the same time? What is going on with me that I am having this type of emotional response? Taking the time to process your emotions and your physical state now gives you more information to work with.

Step Two: Recognize that you always have options.

You just heard something that made you extremely unhappy. But you took control and created options. Do I stay here and continue to feel the way that I feel right now? Do I speak up? Do I disrupt my day and stop whatever is happening in that moment? Or do I simply walk away and remove myself from whatever the circumstances are that caused me to feel the way that I feel? That is what it means to have options and options is power! It is agency! It is freedom! When we practice self-kindness not only are you removing what you don't need but you are adding what is necessary to respond to the external issue appropriately. That is emotional intelligence at its best.

Step Three: Learning to recognize you are not alone.

First recognize that we all have negative emotions happening on the inside of us at times and any of us could experience an emotional outburst at any moment. And when I say everyone. I mean everyone! I bet you remember the incredibly public outburst of one of our favorite actors during one of our favorite award shows when he got to the point where he was no longer happy about the award show host telling jokes at his wife's expense. Talk about, that's it! You are going to live with your aunt and uncle in Belleair! He was angry to the point a physical confrontation occurred. How about Russel Crowe in 2005, Christian Bale in 2009, Reese Witherspoon in 2013, James Cordon in 2022, and a host of others who normally seem to be great people but had a moment of emotional outburst? Face it folks, even with the best of people, sometimes our emotions get away from us. We can't avoid it. It is a part of the human experience. However, knowing that you are not alone in your outburst has great power and can begin the necessary healing to be a better self for yourself. One other remarkable thing about knowing we are not alone is that we then become less inclined to hide our challenges. Often, when we have a temporary lapse in emotional judgement our kneejerk reaction is to run and hide. But when you know you are not the first or the last to do it, you are more than likely to seek out a community of support to help.

CHAPTER VIII

FIND YOUR VILLAGE

Hebrews 10:24-25

> [24] *And let us consider how we may spur one another on toward love and good deeds, 25 not giving up meeting together, as some are in the habit of doing, but encouraging one another—and all the more as you see the Day approaching.*

Earlier in the book, I talked about self-kindness being a team sport. Let's revisit that in more detail now. For whatever reason, middle school seemed to be a rite of passage by way of violence. It seemed like every week, me, or some other boy I knew was finding ourselves in a fight to the death. I cannot tell you all the reasons why we fought. The reasons varied from you sitting in my chair to me buying the same kind of Nike's they wore. Never mind there are over 1,000,000 copies of the same exact sneakers sold worldwide and at least another 150 other young boys in the same school wearing the same exact sneakers. They decided it would be me to be upset with for wearing the same shoes. I remember one day traveling outside my neighborhood with my friend to go to a fight. This was not a schoolyard fight, this was a, "I'm going to find you during the weekend, and we are going to fight it out in the park" fight.

My friend Richard for whatever reason was determined to walk to another neighborhood to fight some boy who said something he didn't like four days earlier in school. Being the friend that I am, if my friend Richard needed someone to go with him to fight, then I was going to go with him. Even when I knew this made absolutely no sense. But he asked, and so I went with him so he could fight. As we are walking deeper and deeper into the unknown neighborhood, I realized we were starting to be surrounded by unfamiliar faces. Who was there to support the other guy who he was going to fight. They were there to cheer on this other guy and if necessary, help him out. I knew it. Richard knew it, God knew it. And everybody in the park knew that day it was not going to go very well for Richard or me because I decided to be with him. So, there we were. Richard was about to fight, and in one last desperate moment I looked up to see if we could find maybe one or two familiar faces. And would you believe me if I told you that there wasn't one or two familiar faces, but more like 10, 15, and 20 other young men who had heard where were going and decided to show up too. Somehow the word got out that Richard was going to be in a fight in a neighborhood outside of our home, and instead of waiting to hear the horrible results, they decided to come and support him as well. We had our numbers, and the other guy had his numbers. And because there were so many unfamiliar faces on both sides, they both decided to call the fight off. Now, for those of you who may not be a Christian, a Buddhist, a Muslim, or follow any religion but simply believe in good luck, I will simply say we got lucky. But more than luck, a greater lesson learned that day, was the importance of village. Growing up, my grandmother used to always say it takes a village to raise a child.

When she said it, she was talking about the various people who could speak life into you and give you wisdom so you would grow up to be a healthy minded man or woman. But in this case the village it took didn't raise us but saved us. When it comes to self-kindness, having a village is everything. Having a group of individuals who are willing to encourage you, inspire you, correct you when it is necessary is important. But also having a community that acts as a safe haven for you to experiment, test, and stretch yourself, is equally vital. On that day, the village showed up to support Richard and I and it didn't stop there. All throughout my life, I have found that I needed a village of persons who would just show up and be there for me. When I needed a sounding board, a listening ear, a faithful breast to keep my secrets, to help me work some things out, the village was right there with me. If you have not yet developed a village of support, here are just a few ways you can find your village. In my journey to find a village, I encountered some interesting people. If you are not a person that likes new experiences, then I don't recommend you jump out there and start meeting people. But I did and it was a blast. For example, I met someone who was really into Bondage. Now, of course, I heard of it, but I never thought about it. But for some reason, her interest interested me, so I asked her how to learn more about it. She opened her laptop and went to a website. Within five minutes of this room talking about the thrill of chains, cages, and other experiences, I knew that they were not my village. No judgement. But not mine. Before you find your village, let me give you a few things to consider.

1. If money was an issue, write down what you like to do.

2. Find out what you don't like to do.

3. Ask yourself why your current friends and associates are your current friends.

4. Identify what your social circles are. If you don't have any, then ask yourself why.

5. Get a YELP account and type in what you think you might be interested in and go visit.

Doing these five simple steps will help lead you in the direction in finding your village. I want to challenge you to begin developing one today. Just start with one person and begin to develop that relationship. Before you know it, you will have to create multiple villages of people to grow with.

CHAPTER IX

I LOVE YOU,
BUT I LOVE ME MORE

Psalm 8:4

> *⁴ what are human beings that you are mindful of them,   mortals that you care for them?*

Anyone who really knows me knows I love reading. Sitting in my room in my comfortable chair listening to music and reading brings me incredible joy. But if I am honest, it was not always the case. Like many children with working parents, I was not always supervised at home. Not that I was by myself, but my grandmother who lived with us, was not always able to watch or play with us as much as she wanted. So, she would sometimes place us in front of a television to keep us preoccupied. Now before you call protective services or judge her for neglect, let me just say it was not for hours at a time. But it was enough time that I developed an obsession for certain shows. No matter what else I had planned to do, I made sure I was in front of my television to watch Super Friends, The Planet of the Apes, and Batman. If television addiction is real, I was undoubtedly an addict by the time I was ten.

My obsession with certain shows continued throughout my teenage and college years. Even when I developed a passion for books, first through the necessity to finish my homework and later for the pure joy of it, I still found certain shows I would watch religiously. One particular show I watch now as an older adult is Chicago P.D. Why? I'm not really sure. I have only visited Chicago a few times in my life and if you were to ask me my favorite things to do there, they would be limited to eating pizza from Giordano's, walking along Michigan Avenue, and eating popcorn from Garratts. That's it! But I love the show even though it's pretty much like other inner-city cop shows. With one exception. The writing is excellent. I often learn really good life lessons from the actors' perspective in the show. For example, there was this one episode where the theme was one person willing to risk their life for someone who didn't care about them. It was obvious from the beginning that this individual was in a one-sided relationship, and ultimately, they lost their life holding on to the thought that one day the love they gave would be reciprocated. In the episode's final scene, two other police officers sit and reflect on the experience and as they reflect, Captain Voight shares in his typical "matter of fact" tone, "It's alright sometimes to let go. It doesn't mean you don't love the other person. It just means you love yourself too."

What an incredible lesson about self-kindness. Being kind to others doesn't mean being unkind to yourself. In fact, it starts with being kind to yourself. Borrowing a quote from the Random Act of Kindness Foundation, "Kindness is doing what you can, where you are, with what you have." In other words, you can't give to someone else what you don't have in the first place. Sometimes the best thing you can do is find ways to be kind to yourself first. That may mean before doing it for others to feel good about themselves, you get your hair or nails done, writing yourself a love note about the cool things you like about yourself, or simply looking at your reflection in a window and smiling. Unfortunately, we live in a world that often requires that you prove to others that you are kind by doing for someone else more than for yourselves.

Often, people love to quote to you the Golden Rule of "Treat others like you want to be treated" or, in the religious world, quote Luke 6:31, "Do to others as you would have them do to you." While both sayings represent a high form of altruism, I believe the bigger lesson is the "as you treat yourself" part. Yep. That part. Before you can treat anyone else with kindness, we should treat ourselves kindly. You cannot treat another person kindly and abuse yourself simultaneously. But how often do we neglect our needs for the sake of others? Now if you struggle with the concept of treating yourself kindly first, then it may seem to you that I am promoting selfishness or self-centeredness so allow me to paint a picture of what I mean. Imagine that you are a glass. In your glass is water that represents kindness that was poured into you a long time ago. One day you come across another glass (a person) and notice their container is empty, so you share some of what you have. That is very noble of you, and you have certainly helped them. The problem arises, however, when you run into another empty glass and another empty glass. One by one, you pour a little out to others while neglecting to refill your cup. Eventually, you will run out of water, and now neither you nor the people you want to be kind to will have what they need. Now imagine before filling others you kept refilling your glass with water (Kindness) first and shared the overflow with others? This is what I mean by being kind to yourself first. The more you are kind to yourself, the more you have to give others through the overflow. In this way, being kind to yourself is not a selfish act but a selfless act of sharing an overflowing, never-ending abundance of kindness with others.

49

CHAPTER X

COURAGEOUS-KINDNESS

Joshua 1:9

> *⁹ Have I not commanded you? Be strong and courageous. Do not be afraid; do not be discouraged, for the Lord your God will be with you wherever you go."*

Being kind takes courage. Houston Kraft, co-creator of R.A.K.A., once wrote, "Everyone craved kindness." Though I agree with Kraft's assessment of the hunger we all have to receive kindness, I often wonder if we know how to express kindness to others beyond a simple act of kindness. Could we show kindness to others that at the same time put us in a vulnerable position? Let me explain what I mean by using my friend Tabitha. She once shared with me how she exercised self-kindness using what I call "courageous kindness." For years, Tabitha suffered from insecurities. Like most of us, her insecurities could be traced back to her childhood. Tabitha recalls, like other children, when she reached the age where she could choose her own outfits. From the colors she chose, and the odd-looking footwear she had on, she began to announce to the world she had arrived at the age of critical fashion decision-making.

Her mother told her a week ago that on the first day of school, she would get to choose her outfit and before the day began, she recalls waking up extra early to start the process of clothing herself. She stayed up all night, planning everything from undergarments to outerwear, shoes, and accessories. And then there she was. Ready to show the world her bright red jumper, lime green shoes. brown belt, and Cowboy hat. With outfit complete, and she ran into her parent's room to display her fabulousness. Unfortunately, what Tabitha didn't know, and her mother could not have prepared for, was the scream and laughter her mother gave at the surprise her daughter planned. Not that her mother was being intentionally mean, she just did not have any idea that her daughter had it in her to be so creatively bold. So instead of encouraging Tabitha to exercise her inner fabulous self and perhaps guide her to develop a slightly more sensible outfit for school, her outburst scared the little girl that would later grow into an extremely conservative and insecure woman because of the traumatic event. Tabitha said for most of her teenage and adult years, she dressed in dark clothes that served as a camouflage than a fashion statement. Not only did she tone down her clothes, but she toned down herself. She became timid and would barely spoke above a whisper. In school, she was the one that sat in the back and would break into cold sweats whenever her teacher called on her. As an adult, she had the desire to work in a field where her intelligence and skills could be displayed and help others succeed.

But because she was so insecure about her looks, she would only apply for jobs which where she worked alone and would go unnoticed. Well, one day, after reflecting on the underwhelming trajectory of her life because of her childhood experience, she decided to get vulnerable and engage other people through acts of kindness. She started surrounding herself with positive people who would in turn encourage her. She also joined a gym, took public speaking classes, and became an active volunteer at her church. She worked hard to change from the insecure person she was to become the person she always knew she could be.

A year after refocusing, an interesting discovery happened. She realized through her networks, counselor, and social activities that she was far from alone in her former insecurities. She met many men and women who suffered through years of insecurity because of someone's reaction to their physical appearance. Many had similar experiences and didn't realize the negative impact, and others had completely different experiences with the same results. So, one day, Tabitha decided to do something for herself, hoping others would support her. For an entire month, she recreated the outfit she wore as a child and proudly wore it everywhere she went. Whether at work, church, the movies, or just hanging with friends, she wore every color, shoe, and accessory just like that day. "On the first day, some people laughed, others celebrated her, and still others just stared and shook their heads. At first, I was embarrassed. I thought to myself, I must have lost my mind to put myself in this position." But after the third day, the stares and jeers no longer bothered her. People went from staring to asking why she was wearing the outfit, and when she proudly shared her experience with them, they began to share their experiences with her." Tabitha's courageous act of kindness to herself to break the bondage of her own insecurities had a ripple effect. in her courageous self-kindness act to overcome her insecurities, she also showed kindness to others by giving them the courage to express theirs.

Merlinda Bobis wrote, "Kindness cannot self-isolate. It moves both ways and all ways, like breath." Tabitha's act of courageous self-kindness could not be contained. It burst forth like a raging sea for everyone to witness. And once seen, people desired to have it for themselves. I have been reading, living, and contemplating the acts of kindness for a while now and if I am honest, I am not sure I have come close to capturing the many sides self-kindness. For example, sometimes kindness can mean being totally selfless for the benefit of another. Paul says in Romans 12:3 that we are not to think more highly of others than we do ourselves. For those, who have not spent years going to Sunday school, catholic school, seminary, and learning the different interpretations of that one passage, allow me a moment to add my thoughts to the volumes of books that covers this passage.

First, Paul was one of the more selfish characters in the bible. His early years were spent persecuting others for having a different belief than his. He was also the coat boy for murderers. It is true. Check it out. Paul what was first known as Saul, had all the education one could obtained, traveled the world as he knew it, and received approval from all the dignitaries of the time. One could say Paul was a man about town and very few people could compete with his level of pedigree. With all that Paul had listed on his resume, it would not be hard to believe that he was an arrogant man. It would also not be hard to believe that he thought he was above most other people. But here in this passage, he tells us that we should not be like he was. We should be the exact opposite of all that he was and all that he was capable of. I share this to help you get a picture of how enormous an ask it was for Paul to make. He was coming from a position of power, authority, and influence and saying the greatest power we could ever have, is showing kindness to someone by thinking they were above us. WOW!

Talk about putting yourself in a vulnerable position. What a display of courageous kindness. In my lifetime I have done some really kind things for others. I have loaned money, helped old ladies cross the street, assist a child with homework, listened to the most gregarious people you will ever meet, and forgiven people wo have intended to cause me harm. But one of the most difficult things I have ever attempted was looking at someone and saying to myself, they are better than me. Now, when I say they are better than me. But is that what Paul meant? Or did he mean, see someone else as if you had no other choice but to see them in a regal position. For example, I am not a Donald Trump fan.

I am not here to make a political point or to speak negatively about his party affiliation. I have known Mr. Trump's ways long before he ran and won the presidency. Being a native New Yorker, I have long been aware that Mr. Trump's practices have been notorious for years before he hit the political scene. So, I do not particularly like many of his views. However, while he was president, if I were to walk into a coffee shop and he was in there, I would instantly give him the respect of the office. I would go as far to say I would give him the respect deserving of his office without even thinking about it. It would happen naturally and instantly. I believe Paul was saying that we are to be kind to others by developing a mindset that when we look at other people, we instantly give them the honor, respect, and even admiration they deserve as being members of the human race. Whew. What would that look like if we developed that type of courageous kindness where we instantly and naturally saw people with that level of honor? I imagine it would mean that we would treat one another differently.

CHAPTER XI

HONEST KINDNESS

John 8:32

32 Then you will know the truth, and the truth will set you free."

There we sat, about to end our marriage, and at the calmest point of what seemed like a four-hour conversation, it hit me. We have been living a lie. Not the kind of lie you see on T.V. where there is some overly dramatic scene where one person finally confesses that they have been living a secret life. But as shocking and revealing as the best day time soap opera ever made. In that moment, I realized that we were living a lie as a couple because I had been lying to myself way before I met her. Years ago, before I met my ex-wife a good friend and I were at lunch, and for some reason we used our time together to share dating insights we had learned as single people. In the midst of the ice-cold margaritas and French fries my friend tells me to remember when you start dating again that everyone interviews well. She said, when you first meet someone and quite possibly months afterwards, the person's goal is to present the absolute best of themselves as possible. They will always try to dress nice even when they are attempting to dress casually, only order the most acceptable dishes on dates, and study current events to appear informed and relevant.

When some people date, they will attempt to be transparent, but only share enough to be interesting and not to the point where they will risk a flight or fight response. As I reflected on that conversation, it occurred to me that I had spent the last twelve years interviewing in my marriage. I worked hard in making sure that my transparency was only as transparent as I could bare. I walked on eggshells trying to say the right things, do the right things, and live up to an impossible example of what it meant to be a man and a husband. All the while, not really knowing it, I was living a secret identity. Secret not only to her, but to me as well. Years ago, I developed a defense mechanism that protected me from the hurt of rejection. From the clothes I wore, the books I read, to even the friends I had, everything in my life was carefully designed to create an image of myself that I wanted to present. In doing so, I hid the insecure, flawed, uncertain me that really wanted to be known and cared for. Am I the only one? Am I the only person that has consciously or subconsciously created a persona that was really not who you were? Author John Powell suggests that we do this because of fear of rejection. But over time the type of ego defense that causes us to pretend to be someone else ultimately places us in a prison and the real you will never be released. Being kind to yourself happens when we are honest with ourselves. Taking time to really learn your likes and dislikes, your fears and what really makes you happy is not an easy thing.

It requires courage and patience and an awareness that what you may discover about yourself is not a very likable person at first. However, over time, you will begin to really appreciate who you are and develop a desire to share who you have discovered with others. Honest-Kindness requires openness with yourself and also being available to all the beautiful things that makes you who you are. The good news is that all of you is quite amazing. The good, the not so good, the fear, and the boldness is all beautiful. Biologist marvel at the complexity and simplicity of the human body. Chemist marvel at how the elements of the periodic table function to describe your inner being. Doctors study for years and still only scratch the surface of how the body is able to heal itself. Counselors constantly update their understanding of the human mind and our behaviors as they discover something new every time they encounter someone. Even spiritually, writers throughout the ages are amazed at the wonders and magnificence of humanity. Now if all of them can see how beautiful you are, then what's stopping you? Even David writes to God in Psalm 139:14 after contemplating his existence, "I will praise thee; for I am fearfully and wonderfully made: marvelous are thy works; and that my soul knoweth right well." Yet, ask almost anyone to tell the "truth" about themselves, and they will quickly point out every flaw they can find to describe who they are. It reminds me of a game we would play as children called the dozens. The rules of the game were simple. Find a flaw whether real or imagined about your opponent and highlight it in such a way that they would feel demeaned, and the audience entertained. As children, we would play this game for hours doing our best to create the funniest observation in hopes of crushing our opponent. Till this day, I cannot tell you why we had so much enjoyment in doing this brutal and cruel game. But what I can tell you is that I was horrible at it. I can recall entire summers where my friends and I would engage in the dozens and day after day I would go home feeling depressed because my friends would identify and highlight a flaw for everyone's amusement.

To make matters worse, over time, I not only became worse at having a witty comeback from the torture, but I also began to internalize and see false flaws in myself. I got to the place where I did not need to play dozens with anyone else. I became a master of playing the dozens alone. Every flaw I saw or imagined became real for me and over the years, they were no longer a laughing matter. They were my reality. I learned to hate myself. As I shared earlier, being kind to ourselves starts with being honest. Telling the truth to yourself about where you are, how you feel, your dreams and desires helps you to later identify the things you need and don't need in order to fully grow. The challenge comes, however, when your "truth" is not true at all, but a detailed compilation of hurt, criticism, derogatory view of yourself. Let's be honest. We all do that to some degree, but some of us have become masters of identifying everything wrong with ourselves. But starting today, we are changing the narrative we believed and the self-loathing habits we have mastered, and we are taking steps to love ourselves and others. Unless you have been living under a rock, you have noticed that diversity is an integral part of our world. Growing up in Brooklyn N.Y., we used the word diversity very differently than it is used today. In fact, as diverse as we were in my neighborhood, we rarely used the term to describe one another. We used "different." When we said someone was different, it wasn't connected to their gender, race, culture, nationality of origin, or sexual preferences. Different simply meant that you were weird. You did not look like us in terms of our dress. You were different if you didn't like Run DMC, or you didn't like the X-men comic books. But today, if you dared called someone different, you risk being sued or cancelled or much worse. So now, we just say it is a diverse community. But whatever you call it, we are living in a very diverse-rich world and with great diversity comes great responsibility.

What you say to one person may be perceived as a compliment and at the same time it can be taken as an insult to someone else. The statements we use to express endearment amongst our compadres could land you with a lawsuit if used with a stranger. No need for me to give you an example. Just open your eyes and you will see them everywhere. What use to be okay in one community has all been banned in another. More than ever, we need to acknowledge the great diverse world we live in and work even harder on being kind to others and ourselves.

CHAPTER XII

CAN I SEE ME NOW

Proverbs 11:17

> *[17] Those who are kind benefit themselves, but the cruel bring ruin on themselves.*

If, by now, you don't see that I am a firm believer in treating others well, then you have not been reading and this book, like so many others, is just sitting on your table to impress your friends. I absolutely believe that we all need to be kind to one another. I also believe, however, that without the practice of self-kindness, being kind to others will be false and unauthentic. Self-kindness in a diverse world means to love yourself so much that even when others mistakenly or intentionally try to offend you, that you will be so loved by you, that you can respond without malice or retaliation. Our leaders globally, nationally, and locally would go further in leading us if they learned this lesson. How many times have you read or heard of wars starting only because someone offended their nation. Why do people have to die because someone did not give you the respect you thought you deserved? As absurd as that sounds, it happens in our world every day. But what would it look like, if instead of overreacting to our differences, we responded with acknowledgment and affirmation of our differences? Because you are awesome!

As we come the conclusion of this book, I want to try my best right now to point out why you are different. You are different because the One who created you decided that you would be one of a kind. You are different because your life experiences and how you respond to them are all your own. You are different because you entered this world like no one else from no one else at the exact time you entered the universe. You are different because you have read this book and hopefully, with me, decided to love yourself like no other living being on the planet or beyond can.

I have a vision statement for myself that I have on every electronic device I own. You can find it on the walls, and on several post-it notes around my office. As a part of my daily practice, I make sure to read it and I ask myself if what I am doing is in line with what I believe about myself. I ask myself if these words are truly a part of the goals I have set for the day, week, month, and year? It simply says,

"I have a strong desire to love God, myself, and others very well."

When I read my vision statement it helps me prioritize. When I read my statement, it gives me a pattern to live my day and my life by. When I read my statement, it encourages me to keep moving forward, even when I fail. I invite you to write your own and put it everywhere your eyes gaze. It can be whatever you want but try your best to add "you" in it. Because frankly, the world needs you and you are worth remembering that fact every day of your life. I love you dearly, but greater than that, you love you and God loves you more.

ABOUT THE AUTHOR

 As the lead pastor of The Village in Desoto Texas, Dr. Keith L. Somerville draws from his experiences in ministry to inspire others to prioritize their well-being through seeking God, and looking within to discover purpose, set priorities, and live a more fulfilled life.

He holds a degree from Morehouse College, Gammon Theological Seminary (ITC), a Doctorate from Emory University and is also certified in Clinical Pastoral Education.

"**I Fix Me**" encourages readers to focus on what truly brings happiness and live in the overflow of self-kindness, ultimately fostering a more compassionate world. When not hanging out with people at a local coffee shop, he loves reading, meditating, writing, watching movies, and riding his motorcycle.